Inner Child: "Runner"

Kori Lee

Presentation by *BookLeaf Publishing*

Web: www.bookleafpub.com

E-mail: info@bookleafpub.com

ISBN: 9789357444897

First edition 2023

*The one in my dreams, the one my bones cannot
shake, my bluebird.*

PREFACE

"Cover me up- know your enough-to use me for good."- Jason Isbel

You are the King in all of my writings.

Inner Child

My hearts inside my head
Something I should not ever do
Drowned in blood and left for dead
Inner child can't seem to get used to

The whys the how's the when's
Story lines that never quite add up
Sensitive - truths hiding lies
Soon enough I'll call the bluffs

Collecting all the cards won't know til then
The things I've known
Biding time collecting pieces
Omissions seeking shelter in unknowns

intention makes no match for intuitions
For I can be an actress too
Hidden talents for protection
A lover should need not to have to use

Why must a trust be broken
Given no chance to have a voice
Burnt out in my exhaustion
Knowing My inner child
had not choice

Why would a mute kept lover
even think to go to war
Soon after peace- will come another
Ponder on -what I'd be fighting for

Exhale to keep me grounded
Whirlwinds from all I feel
Like a dreidel spinning faster
Cannot convince me they're not real

Scales that balance on statistics
Research done all on my own
Odds diminish like a spirit
That in another builds a home

experimenting mixing traumas to dissolve
The walls I've built
No solution I've discovered can erase
The Shame & guilt

Can't blame a heart for trying
In desperation I've learned much
I never want to be a shadow
Or dare -think to let -another touch

The inner child in my closet
I've ached and ached to set her free
Yet there she sits -softly rocking
Clung to an ever shaking pair of knees

Pit of my stomach wants so badly
To show her that there's safety in a hug
And that the people who've made her doubt it
We're simply too
incapable of love

Beg her to burn the pillow
that's gathered all her silent screams
Help her see that she's been triggered
From all the less than kinder falsities

Transitioned from the mouths of those she's
trusted
to a place inside her head
Bellowing in constant echos
Show her to silence them instead

Back from the grips of death id peel her
Have her look me in the eyes
Cure the panic felt seeing- into someone
Reassure- her fight or flight

That it has more than served a purpose
But now it's time to let her free to roam
Then show that lost & broken child
How to love herself back home

Riptide

There's a secret in the riptide
Inland from the wounds and bones
Like a sunken buried treasure
With no map for getting home

My head and heart they collide
The winner rests on fate
For I can't complete a sane thought
Can't make sense of anything

Push and pull to find the answers
The moon is playing games
For she controls the waters
Decides how calm or violent to make waves

I feel her energy within me charging me back
when I'm depleted
Currents soften as they near me
Has mercy on me once defeated

There's a secret in the riptide
A secret you may never tell
So many ways to fall in love
While some have tripped
Others fell

Me I dig both hands in
Submerse
then dive into depths
Deeper than the pits of hell
In search of treasure hidden
The love I seek lays there on ocean floor
Amongst forgotten shells

The ways my mind is broken opposes
My blueprint for connection
Never quite fitting together
Full of empty contradictions

There's a secret in the riptide
If you listen close the truth is there
In oceans I easily hide
When the moon's not playing fair

Strings

I had to learn the hard way
Sometimes it makes a difference to say
How you really feel
Your still on my mind every Sunday
a ritual we chose consistently & you'd stay
the night after gigin' on my side of town
Our reset day
I see you're still more lost than found

Do I even cross your mind?
- you made One hell of big leap
Strung me out like a puppet
Didn't keep
All the promises nobody made you
Fuckin make me
You kept denying it the same

Never having any accountability
You won't see how you
Completely shattered me
roundabouts wear me out
Placing blames

on popsicle sticks
Holding up strings

Felt like you enjoyed the puppeteering
Words cut straight through all my sensitive
Feelings
Yours left as quickly as they came

up until this day I've never held a lover like you
Don't have the words to say -Do you regret
things too?
Ever wish you woulda stayed?
Couldn't make you turn in your runnin' shoes
Laced them up to chase your fame

You still cross my mind but I realized somethin'
Those memories they don't mean nothin'
Here to keep my bluebird in a cage
Clipped wings
While your playing center stage
Singing
Your songs of better days
Oh It's time to turn the page

I refuse to be stuck on things you didn't say
When You turned from me to walk away
Not much the type to beg you stay
Never wanted you to go
I know you had to know
I only wanted you to grow
I guess it had to be this way
But you still come around every Sunday

I'll learn how to drown your memory out
Let my heartache dissipate
I can manage to feel hope maybe one day
I'll find peace that you can't shake
I'll open up the cage
This bluebird I'll set free
You'll see
A different side of me
A side You'll never touch to break

Don't wanna ever know a lover quite like you
Guess that's the point I'm getting to
I'd rather not cross paths with you
The day I do will be too soon
I wish you'd go away
Give back my town and give me space
This town won't take you any place
You never liked to feel disgraced
It always is the nights you play
Regretting the next day
Why can't you just stay away
I never needed to learn it the hard way
it won't make a difference
You didn't stay
The truth rings loud and clear
So why are you still playing here
Holdin' your guitar and a beer
Tell me
why are you still playing here?

Soaring Skies

My heart seems to have grown some wings
It's soaring up and high
And all around the rubble
Others left on dangled time

My heart was full of icey things
No one could get inside
Then all you did was sing to me
So fast you felt so right

So sing to me my bluebird
Never break the bonds of trust
Love me til our souls are free
And know that you're enough

To capture my affections
For I will hold your heart in mine
in our laughing- make connections
Stronger than the usual kind

The nights we cry in laughter
Like Magnets pulling me In close
The things my heart feels after
Words could never help you know

Sing to me sweet bluebird
Tell me all the things you long for
I'll set free what I can manage to
And hope it's what you live for

Kiss my lips and whisper good night things
then trace your way around
Each and every scar I hold
Before we both lay down

But know before your dreams take hold
My heart has grown some wings
I'll soar around while making home
In all your darkest things

Sleep well my darling blue bird
I'll be here when you wake up
Each day I fall more for you
As I soar the skies of love.

I Think Of You

I think of you each day break
Before each day breaks me
I think of all the moments
And all the cherished memories

I think of you each evening When I hanker for
your soul
When I'm friendless, feeling lonely, when a
secrets needing told

I'm weak and I'm tormented
Oh how easy I could fade
Into each and every demon
I see melting you away

Do not think for a moment
That I don't grieve and I dont ache
For we've been true to each other
And that friendship none could fake

I've cried so many nights
I feel so guilty that I shake
But I have to choose my freedom
Because my freedoms whats at stake

To me your heart is golden and to know it I've
been blessed
I'll cherish it from where I sit
I haven't lost hope yet

That you will too find healing - in a world
Gone dark and cold
That you'll remember all your value
Without needing to be told

Please know I pass no judgement for we're all
just dangling
On a tightrope of our traumas
Ones that barely let us breathe

I'd never tell a secret nor would I betray
A friend
No matter how time passes or no matter what
our sins

You may think of me a stranger because I know
how time, it fades
But you have my love and loyalty
Please know - I'll take it to my grave

I hope one day I find you and I hope one day
you're free
From the chains I feel that bind you
The chains I beg you see

For I know that when you break them
You will soar so high and far
Until then- I'll hold you quietly
Like a bluebird in My heart

Forgotten Your Tattoos

I can not for the life of me remember your
tattoos
Not vaguely shapes or colors
Maybe Im finally getting over you

The imprint of your auras fading
I have to close my eyes to find a familiar trace
Of your scent when you'd just showered
Above your cheek on your sweet face

The essence of the person loving me
Was almost intoxicating
You'd walk up to let me smell it
Smile at me patiently waiting

Inhaling our connection you would beam, and
you'd just stand
Until I'd do that thing That'd I'd do after
Collapse & melt into your hands

You'd laugh like you were proud to let me
If I forgot you'd walk right up and grin
Leaning in and wait until I'd see how fresh and
clean you were - there's nothing that I wouldn't
give

To remember that smell clearly on days like
today
where I hurt and struggle
Because I'm starting to forget those little things
We shared with one another

Like when I felt you looking at me I would look
up and catch your gaze
I loved how you would watch me How you
would seem to be amazed

Id pretend Not to take notice so I could feel your
eyes on me a little longer
Or I'd say what? And you'd say nothing
Or say your love was growing stronger

Sometimes those blue eyes watered
I'd ask what was wrong and you'd answer soft
That you really loved me truly
You'd wonder how we'd found this kind of love

I can't explain it but I saw in your eyes a flicker
like I could see deep in your soul
I let myself believe it -& in that flicker
The one that promised me together we'd grow
old

I'm fond of those moments where our eyes
would meet those moments where you'd let me
see
The man beneath the armor beginning to
Embrace his vulnerability's

I'd give my eyes to feel yours on me
If one more time you'd look at me that way
And when the time came for our eyes to meet
I would never look away

When my dreams don't let me sleep
Late at night Sometimes I cry & ache for you
I wonder if you think of me and If your
forgetting all our little love things too

The little moments we shared, my smell, my
laugh, my face,the taste,
Of true loves kiss on lips you kissed, each tattoo
and where each is placed

I'll never understand no matter how hard I have
sincerely and certainly been trying
Come the end I had no say in, how you could
just leave me that way hurting & crying

Alone and so abandoned - why did you awaken
all the love in me
With no intent of loving "more than"
Gave us up so easily

I know that feelings change sometimes but that's
where I'm most offended
Just days before you shut me out
You swore we'd always mend it 10

If I had thought you capable, felt a spec of doubt
you'd armor up when hardship came
I truly never would have put my walls down
Or let you look at me that way

So cold and so collected you argue like I wasn't
there as a witness to these things
You make up rules, betray connections that I
cannot be imagining

If your heart and mind decided- felt they loved
me less than- instead of more
That you no longer felt the level of attachment
you claimed you felt before

You shouldn't have misled me, made my pain an
inconvenience of your time
Because how fair do you think that would be
After not valuing mine?

You didn't back out slowly like people who have
human doubts and fears will do
You simply pulled the trigger- bullets I myself
handed to you

Hurt people they hurt people and when there is
fear the monsters come
I just wish there was acknowledgment Why
deny what you have done

You became everything I feared the most
Then defended all the ways you hurt me
knowing hurt was all that it could bring
Claimed to have changed feelings which I never
sensed
-Knowing that I've always had a gift or curse for
noticing

So if your math of 2+2 adds up to 5
I rest my case on my right to be utterly confused
the math just won't add up no matter how
frustrated and annoyed the facts make you

A plus b = it gets you C why can't you see - the
answer's- always love and that's
the only rule
You can carry on in denial & - keep breaking
things
But that makes you the fool

But The second time makes it a choice
I've not forgot- I have my choice as well
That mask you wear won't love you
Neither will I- because-
I'll soon forget your smell

Ill find a way to make this heart stop loving you
stop replaying ways you pointed out to me that I
was not enough
When you were grasping straws for excuses so
you'd feel justified in how inhuman you felt
fitting-
to strip me of your love

Attitude that felt not empathy, not giving credit
to all that you inflicted
Bringing irrelevancies up like they warranted or
evened things giving you redemption

Can you honestly compare those things as if you
give them equal ground
I'd have never let those circumstances
Silence you so cruelly- but I guess that's why
I've found

Peace in the confusion, though it's not much
consolation for my used and lied to heart
The one you let sit dying lonely
After ripping it apart

You were the best thing, you were all that is
good-too.
I miss watching while you sang to me
Now I've forgotten your tattoos

I Never thought it possible that you'd leave me
hurt and feeling used
But I cannot for the life of me - remember your
tattoos

Giving Tree

I'd like to write a song for you
You'd see how far I'd go
tell ya best I know how to
Of all the things I know

You see I've got a problem
A sort of writers block
Tongue sits still
Because this kind's
The kind that jumbles thoughts

But if I wrote a song for you
A story it would tell
Of how you went to war with demons
And revived my wishing well

Drought had plagued the core of who
I used to think I was
You watered me with confidence, in truth , with
trust, for love.

You fed my favorite bluebird
You sang me Melodies
You sparked a dying passion
That burned my weeping willow tree

You then dug into cooling ashes
And one by one you planted seeds
Begun to water passions
New roots took hold in me

You Coaxed the sun to melt away
The fortress I hid in
Then you began examining
Each flaw and every sin

I guess I grew too rapidly
It seems the more I grew
You began To water doubt in me
Then cut down our love so true

Light a match and burn me
Then one of us may live
From the heat, the lies, the promises
It's my last gift to give

For You Make My Nightmares Tremble

I think I have awoken -From a grave and fearful
sleep
Where nightmares filled with demons took me
deep into the sea

The boat was steady rocking I waited long for
calm
But there was nothing steady
No not this ship that I sailed on

Im certain I was dreaming although I felt the
winds
Heard the rumble from the waves- a warpath to
break Sins

Just as the ship was sinking & with death i made
my peace
I awoke a gentle hand on me
Caressing my release

Confused I lay there frozen paused in what was
true
Then closer moved a burning heart
Mine started burning too

The scars exposed around it-
they seemed Eager -
to give way
As if it was with certainty this strangers heart
would stay

Familiar seemed these hands on me
As they began to roam
I welcomed them effortlessly
And now I'm finally home

Home is where the heart rests
& This home I rest with ease
When terrors From my past
Creep in
This warmth it cannot freeze

Stay a while, hands so sweet, for you make my
nightmares tremble
Trade my hurt and hate for love
A love I'll long remember

Unknown Territory

My wandering feet have wound up in your
unknown territory
I caution we might not jump in unless you like
exploring

For my love is like a hurricane my loyalty is
sound
Lightening in me none will tame
sure feet on solid ground

It seems we have crossed paths in such an
unknown territory
Don't doubt me though - unlike those whom you
may have held before me

My mind protects this heart of mine
For in failures I've learned much
Broken people they break things
So in love- I cannot rush

Now here you stand before me
If you might stay - won't try and guess
In my unknown territory
There's Old trails from those who left

But none yet -have loved exploring
so if you do there's common ground
For I am on a mission
to discover things Unfound

I know we might be traveling in
some unknown territory
Call me yours or call me friend
For now let's keep exploring

Fuck It Up

Why do the waves of grief come in & come
crashing down on me
Never felt this lonely yet I sometimes ache for
what could be

Don't want to fuck it up all that I've touched
seems has surely turned to ashes
Before eyes so far from blind that can't pretend
I'm not observing every action

There's no rewind on aches and pains
A hurting mind can not make sense
No form of justifications I could find
Excuses them

A starving hunger to be seen yet never wanting
to unlock
The door to get inside of me I just let everybody
knock

The repetitions tiring but I still don't open up the
door
Once someone gets inside they break things in
me as if they owned the place before

Is it cold or calculated can't decipher which I am
Either way think I just may be made
to have an empty hand

Life has a funny way of working out
Try to embrace my changing heart
Fighting battles no one sees in me
That tear me into parts

Growing feels like dying seems like I die to die
again
Inner child in me crying solitude is my best
friend

I know there's light, I've walked this tunnel
Always make my own way through
Find ways to find appreciation
In all the aching that I do

My humanness feels lonely yet my spirit is at
fault you see
For the no trespass signs I have in places where
my love once used to be

connected with the moon my tides are changing
getting stronger, knowing
I might not find my home on earth
But I'll try my best to keep On growing

Bargaining

Shade tree

Meet me near our shade tree
eyes took hold like roots, I blushed
The parts of me I'd buried deep
First time I felt "enough"

My sanity sleeps inside a pill
Hindsight is 20/20
Relief each day I swallow it
I can see how you left running

I know now that you had to go
Within, true love - wish you the best
Did my worst to numb this heart since then
From bleeding in my chest

I go back to that November when I melt into my
sleep
Back to that night in Austin
A memory I'll forever keep

Meet me at our shadetree
It's there my soul tied tight to yours
Tried hard to find it after
loves held no candle quite like yours

A year has came and gone - I've gotten good
Wearing this mask
Make no mistake you were my first true love
No doubt in me you'll be my last

First thought when my eyes open and the last
before they fade
Even though no words since spoken
I'll love you til- I'm in my grave

We'll meet again one day &
Until my imagination sets me free
I'll keep bargaining with the universe
That you make way back to me

I Imagine It Goes

Meant to hang the moon for you
The best of best intentions
I left words unsaid hangin instead
But thought Id maybe mention

My heart stayed there with you that day
Just had to chase my passion
Never planned to leave you there that way
My heart and soul were clashing

You cross my mind come wintertime
Some nights I make believe
The life we'd have if id have stayed
You breathing next to me
I swear it wasn't you I ran from
Promise- I was running towards my soul
A year has come and gone away
And times taken it's toll
But like yesterday the memories of
Your smile across the from me
Fill my mind my heart still sore
Your love was hard to leave

I never hung the moon for you
The best Of best intentions though
Put on my wheels and laced my shoes still have
this heart you know
Wish I didn't have to go
Just needed space to grow
Oh how I wish I didn't go
Oh how I wish I didn't go

I Want To Build An Empire

I wanna build an empire
A castle in the clouds
Rise above those uninspired
Nobody order me around

Shared throne to someone worthy
He that sees me deep inside
Doesn't have to yell to tell me that
I needs to wipe my eyes

Love is of the essence
Of Time - beginning now
Don't need another lesson
Slowly letting my walls down

I wanna build an empire
rule long side my king
Passion that is set on fire
Conquer challenges it brings

Look into eyes of certainty
Love that quivers to our bones
Breathing life into each other
Inhaling truths into our lungs

Footprints left upon the earth
That trail right through our fears
Never doubting, or deceiving
As we navigate the years

I'd rather be left to my wildness
In time the loneliness would fade
Than settle for usurpers
That aim to make of me a slave

My heart is for my people
Villages take time and bumpy roads
Learning burning overturning
A queen in me shall grow

Playing House

I tried my best to forget
Move on from loving you
No matter where I turned
I found I knew not what to do
You still echod in my silence
Laughing till my cheekbones sore
I spoke words into my journal
Until I forgot what I hurt for

I still dream of you at present
Sneak in my sleep with no consent
When we meet there I feel sorrow
And many unspoken deep regrets
Wish I'd have loved you freely
So many years I craved Connection
So scared I tripped on my own feet
No focus on my own direction

I clung to my best intentions
Could not accept the things I knew were true
How I was proud you changed directions
Thinking it was good for you
But inside you lost the music
Swear I never meant for it to fade and wilt
Needed to find your own salvation
Not the playing house in love we'd built

I know your heart wanted to stay
Just as bad as head said go
I felt anger when you walked away
I've now since let that ego go
So proud of all the things accomplished
Seems that our love was not in vein
Felt your heart in every season
I know one day we'll meet again
My ears echo your laughter
Haven't touched a crawfish since
I still listen to your music in my car
When I'm not with the kids

I hope life takes you where you dream
And your lyrics leave their mark
On each and every person
That receive some of your heart
Don't forget to thank your maker
you'll need your fists to be unclenched to pray
A plan we'll never understand
Some grief will always stay

Dig deep and pull the light out
All your magic long collected
Watching from a distance I shall be
Til death we'll be connected

If I Had Been

If I had been a sailor I would glide across the sea
In search of but one treasure
Some eyes will never see

For it isn't gold nor gemstones that brings whom
finds it wealth
But Riches that will burst ones soul
And cure a sick mans health

In a form sometimes rejected, by hearts and men
with scars
They Diminish and neglect it
Yet true love outshines the stars

If I had been a farmer I'd watch my garden
bloom
I'd store my efforts harvests
Grow joy that fills a room

Before I'd welcome strangers
To sit with me and feast
This wise surviving farmer
Would know which monsters hide in sheep

But I am not a farmer ground of trust and love
unturned
A lesson- not to water demons
Was a most painful lesson learned

If I had been a scientist, my name spread
through ancient times
As she who cured afflictions
Caused by the most heinous of crimes

Crimes of lust and poisons that the devil forged
himself
And placed into unknowing hearts -minds
weakened, fixed on wealth

Regretful, I'm no scientist I hold no cure or
potion
So I'll sit back while hatred rules
The lands between the oceans

& choose to be another , a lover, and a friend, a
daughter, sister, mother
I'll be them til the end
I carry imperfection, scars, and guilt none but
me know
But even in a dying world
My faith and love will glow

Bright 'longside ambitions, and dreams of all I'll
be
But most of all I'll cherish those whom choose
to cherish me

Pretenders, fools, and monsters
You may knock upon my door
But I'll no longer dine with you
You'll feast on me no more

The seductive tongues of liars- those miserable
by choice
Speak not, nor anchor down to me
You have no weight nor voice

Fierce a woman born from the ashes of her scars
She'll have more reasons to succeed one for
each & every star.

Til It Fades

Not quite as simple as The end -
in re-occurring dreams
Putting trust into another imperfect
and hurting human being

Scales -don't always balance even
Though one should take into account
Scars- exist- though some can't see them
Add too much weight the arms give out

When do you feel the lonely?
What is the threshold til your break?
The point where water cracks foundations
Destroys the dam that hugs the lake

How does one evade ones will?
Conquer a mind as if it's sleeping
Easy as the river flows
Though heavy as a soul that's weeping

Spinning chaos with no control
Tops made not -for standing still
Peace might have the chance at catch-up
If value placed in what was real

Tangible no longer- let it slip through shaky
fingers
Memories hit stronger til my scent no longer
lingers

On the pillows where love rested dreams that
didn't quite take flight
Where truth and trust were bested
Raw mistakes and lonely nights

I'll fade with all the others
though one day I know you'll see
My love unlike another's
Roots of love like cypress trees

I seek the deep you bask in shallows
Lately - tell me why that's changed
Can't speak in truths consistently
Pointless stories re-arrange

I ask too much I argue not
our talking circles spin and spin
Why not agree to disagree
That way we both can take the win

Isn't that what it's about when we play the game
this way
Isn't hard to figure out
The things that make a lover stay

Consistency, conviction, overcoming lonely
nights the space next to the side of you
Not filled with foolishness or spite

Temporary turns to permanent in terms of
damage done
Real life holds no rewinds
That's why the little lonely sun

Inside of you that feels an appetite
Not a single soul could fill
Until the man inside the mirror
Allows himself to finally heal

You can keep wondering in the darkness
Won't find me on the other side
I'll warn a king ends up a joker
Without a queen to sit beside

But who am I to have opinions
When my value comes and goes on whims
That's why my scent will fade from bedsheets
You'll no longer find me in

Memories slip away and taste less bitter
Hearts heal in their own ways
find joy within your freedoms
& love my memory til it fades

Unhinged

Panic setting in usual but unusual self with
fluctuations
Mirror shows someone unhinged
In my consistent inconsistent calculations

Always busy never accomplishing
My list of my honey dos
Body sore , yet finished nothing
By the time the day is through

Can't keep my focus- mind all scattered
What was it I misplaced?
Wasted time to try remembering
Where random things are placed

I put it there so I won't lose it,
Though How contradictory
Moments wasted trying to remember
How secret could it's placement be?

Guess for now - throw in the towel
Frustration makes my eyesight weak
I'll end up more frustrated til I locate the thing I
seek

Traumas -some generational others I have asked
not for
Gaslit, unhinged , emotional
Couldn't find the exit door

Until the damage done messed up the wires to
my brain
Convinced that If I spoke my truth
I'd be a liar anyways

Why is simplicity so costly
need the most basic things to live my life
Water, food, a bed to rest
Maybe someone to love me right

But then again I am unhinged
A burden most won't want to Learn
For it's not theirs to try and concur
A task that isn't their concern

It's hard to make ends meet it's even harder to
see light
Out of the hole you've sunken into
Thanks to your triggered fight or flight

Compulsively impulsive so the grandest of my
plans
Lack ambition for completion
Once redundancy sets in

Can't get into the groove because unhinged
I operate
Not a thing to show for it
Stuck in this tragic state

To feel so happy and so sad is like a bomb
Waiting to boom
The excitement of it Overshadows not -
The damage it will do

My future feels unhinged
Uncertain chaos -seeming grim
Trade anything to understand myself
Surely no one else could comprehend

The misery accompanied with all the most
uncertain paths
Body's weary while my minds unhinged
& stuck inside the past

Noah

inside my vault of memories-
So many shelves- Are filled with you
That night in Austin, Noah singing
Felt like my dreams were coming true
Front row you sat beside me
Watched me dote upon each note
His fingers seamless like I'd dreamed it
Mine were twisted 'round my coat
Cheeks were hurting from my grinning
Goosebumps lingered til the end
The night Our downfall was beginning
Though me so unaware again
In your head you had one foot out
I now know ignorance is bliss
Was this some sort of goodbye plan
A twisted parting gift?
You held me like a cigarette
Never cared much for the end
Never guessed that you'd be leaving
lesson scars so hard to mend
Inside my vault Of memories

I'm clearing room for more
Won't forget that night in Austin
Though it's not you it's cherished for

Noah singing and your hand in mine
I could tell that you were home
So was I - frozen in time
Now in a vault alone

When I Felt Right You Left

When I felt right you left
Reflecting on how One of us seems lost in all
the loss
I don't really have the words
My dear, don't mean to seem so cross

It hurts me when the blows are low
Such absolutes - my ears feel lies
Diminishing my shock - confused
It makes me feel inside

Choose my words careful & true - not to shame
you or offend
Reminding you my love is true
& it's love that always wins

Try to love in your love language
Though God knows I've often struggled
But it's how we take love in that balances
each other

When i felt right you left
Can't imagine no one else but you
Unexpected but not shocked a bit
Broken heart I've grown into

I throw in the towel -Make every word hurt
- so leavins easy
I felt right You left
Misunderstood
Ain't looked back yet- But I regret -
it's never easy

Desert Rose

Incoming gusts of chaos - steadfast winds
whisper the truth
Carrying my tumble weed of memories & scars
Collected from my youth
Across sands of times they ricochct
Not near as light as they appear To be
Hellbent to make of me a bowling pin
Keep Circling back relentlessly
I stand tall like a survivor would
Or might be that I just freeze
Either way I get back up again
Each time I hit my knees
Yet lately I've been wondering
What if I can't find healing
Never been quite this exhausted
Never so sore as I've been feeling
Surviving's not a mode to live in
Temporary it should be
Each passing year that's came & gone
I find strength blooms less in me
Some might see a desert rose
They will never see or comprehend
How many thorns reside inside
This strange flower in the sand

How can I escape the heat when the desert is so
vast
And each time that it rains it seems
Much shorter than the last
Mirages left by leavers
Moving on to greener things
Seems to be the steady story line
My maker has for me
I've tried to note the lessons
While roaming up and down the dunes
Tried to grow so tall and strange
Though, Could never reach the moon
A rose forever stuck within the burning desert
sand
Watching all the tumble weeds that come for me
Too tired now to stand

Roller Coaster Of Dark

It's cold outside my bedroom window
ever more within this battered heart
Frigid air seeps through the seal
Disappointments ringing for on this night
I'm feeling dark

Fearful thoughts creep forward
parts of me numb from every fight
But the rest of me now trembles
changing form beneath moonlight

Im feeling dark can no one see?
Only My echo bounces back
You were the light once leading me
Now far as I can see pitch black

Images of dreadful things broken records
Played on loops
Though I have nearly now forgotten
The warm smooth voice of you

I'm feeling dark just leave me be not that you'd
even turn around to glance
You've stolen priceless things from me
Hardly gave this love a chance

Let's agree to disagree for you'd say you met me
In the middle
But if the judgement solely up to me
I'd say you only tried a little

Fly free bird
if i the cage you think you needed
to break free from
Just let me keep my memories so I might watch
them all as re runs

I'm feeling oh so dark my lover lost
Pained eyes, they cry. You're sound asleep
I sewed my future into yours I guess now
I'm alone & left to reap

I'll tuck my knees in tightly
firmly nailed into My chest
As if metal kissed by lightening
my frantic heart won't take a rest

I'm feeling dark so very dark
this pain unlike any other that I've known
I whimper in my sleep knew better than to make
in you
my home

Why do I feel so dark why did the sound of
music fade
I wish now instead you'd take these memories
I am exhausted from replays

Conversations never spoke out loud
The words that I'd go back and say
Before you broke your promise of forevers
Then chose to burn me at the stake

When did you feel the threat of enemy while
looking at my face
A love I thought not fleeting or possible it be
replaced

I shout from the inside
all the disappointments
ringing clear
lips closed tight
It doesn't matter
Your the only one
id want to care

I'm feeling dark I'm feeling used I'm feeling
every little painful thing
Some linger
some surge through
Some I know will die with me

There must be something wrong with me this
time
I feel no chance i might recover
Put all my stock in loving you in ways
unlike I could love another

How could you give up on me this easy
why have you awakened all the love in me
No intent of being true why turn the lock & keep
the key

My heart will cry out for you forever
I'll read our story front to back
Slowly flipping through the pages though the
ending comes so fast

I'll cherish all the words we've spoken
Though they've fallen short & let me down
I stood a queen that wasn't broken
On my head the perfect crown

Gold and gemstones we had no need for
It was the love we shared that made us rich
So why'd you have to break us down
And why was it done like this

So I'll bathe in all the darkness ride this roller
coaster of emotions

Alternate the hurt and anger that's grown deeper
than the oceans

I feel I've made a fool of me by begging
I'll be a fool for love you see
If that is what would cease the pain I feel
Id drop straight to my knees

I pray for you on rare occasions when I
remember how to pray
Bargaining to go back where I met you
Id love you better make you stay

words left unanswered, me left unseen, you
untouched, & feeling new
This grief in me where love should be
Your Forever must be done & through

You promised me forever I believed it in my
heart and soul
You are my only person
I thought together we'd grow old

I've surely grown to fear my dark
But like clockwork darkness always comes
It wreaks havoc on my heart
Not that much of it is
left to take things from

Stomach twists in knots from when I wake until
I close my crying eyes
Some tears are shed from sorrows
Others from such cold goodbyes

That's the hardest pill you made me swallow
How not only did you try to feed me shit
then you had such nerve to act offended
I didn't like the taste of it

In That moments where I realized
I loved a man trapped in illusions
No harm intended from his lies
He'll see problems never solutions

A dose of pure toxicity when you add a dash of
utter disrespect
Into a caldron throwing in a pinch of all my deep
regrets

Im left mourning whats left over once you were
done with all my flesh
I used to glow, I used to smile , held a beating
heart inside my chest

But now you've been gone for weeks
Some days I feel okay -at best still hurt
& sad

But I've still held hope you might come back for
me
What's left of hope is fading fast

The way you slipped right through my fingers
Disappearing in the wind
Has left a hole inside my heart that
No amount of time will ever mend

I'm feeling dark I'll say again I no there
Can't be confusion or mistaking
You abandoned me so heartlessly
If you loved me you were faking